AF481151

COOL EXPERIMENTS

ON STATIC ELECTRICITY

SCIENCE BOOK OF EXPERIMENTS

Children's Electricity Books

In this book, we're going to talk about some cool experiments you can do to learn about static electricity. So, let's get right to it!

If you've ever walked across a thick, plush carpet by dragging your feet and then you touched a doorknob, you may have felt a spark. That spark was a result of static electricity. If you pull your sweater off really fast, sometimes your hair will stick to the sweater or stick straight up in the air. That's an example of static electricity too! There are examples of static electricity in nature as well. Lightning is actually a very dangerous form of static electricity.

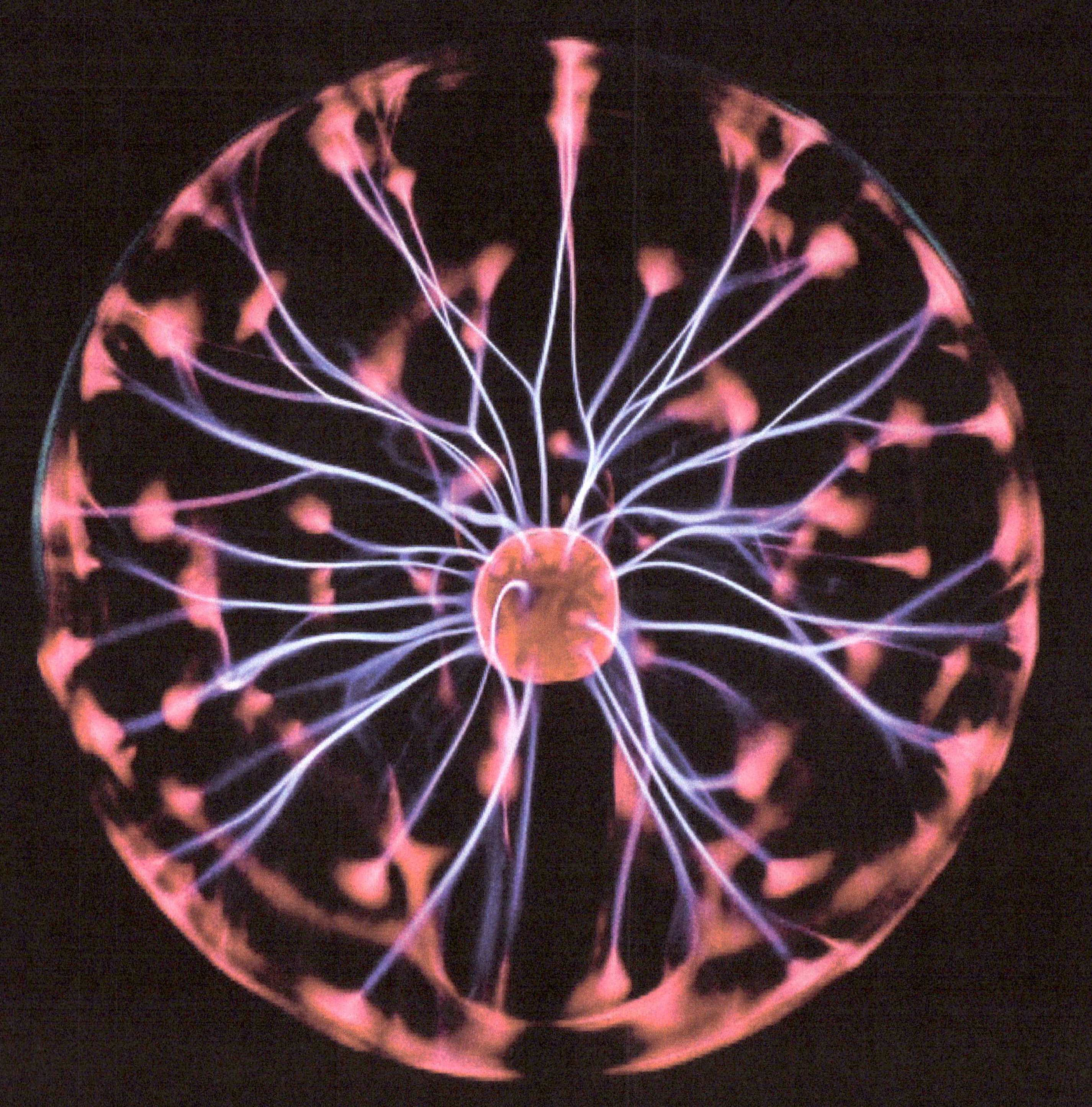

WHAT IS STATIC ELECTRICITY?

Static electricity happens at the atomic level. All matter is made up of atoms that are composed of electrons, which are negatively charged, protons, which are positively charged, and neutrons, which don't have a charge. The neutrons as well as the protons are part of the central core of the atom called its nucleus.

The electrons spin around the nucleus so, depending on the material, they can be more easily dislodged from their atoms. For example, if you rub the surface of a balloon with a cloth very quickly, it will build up a charge of electrons, which have negative charges.

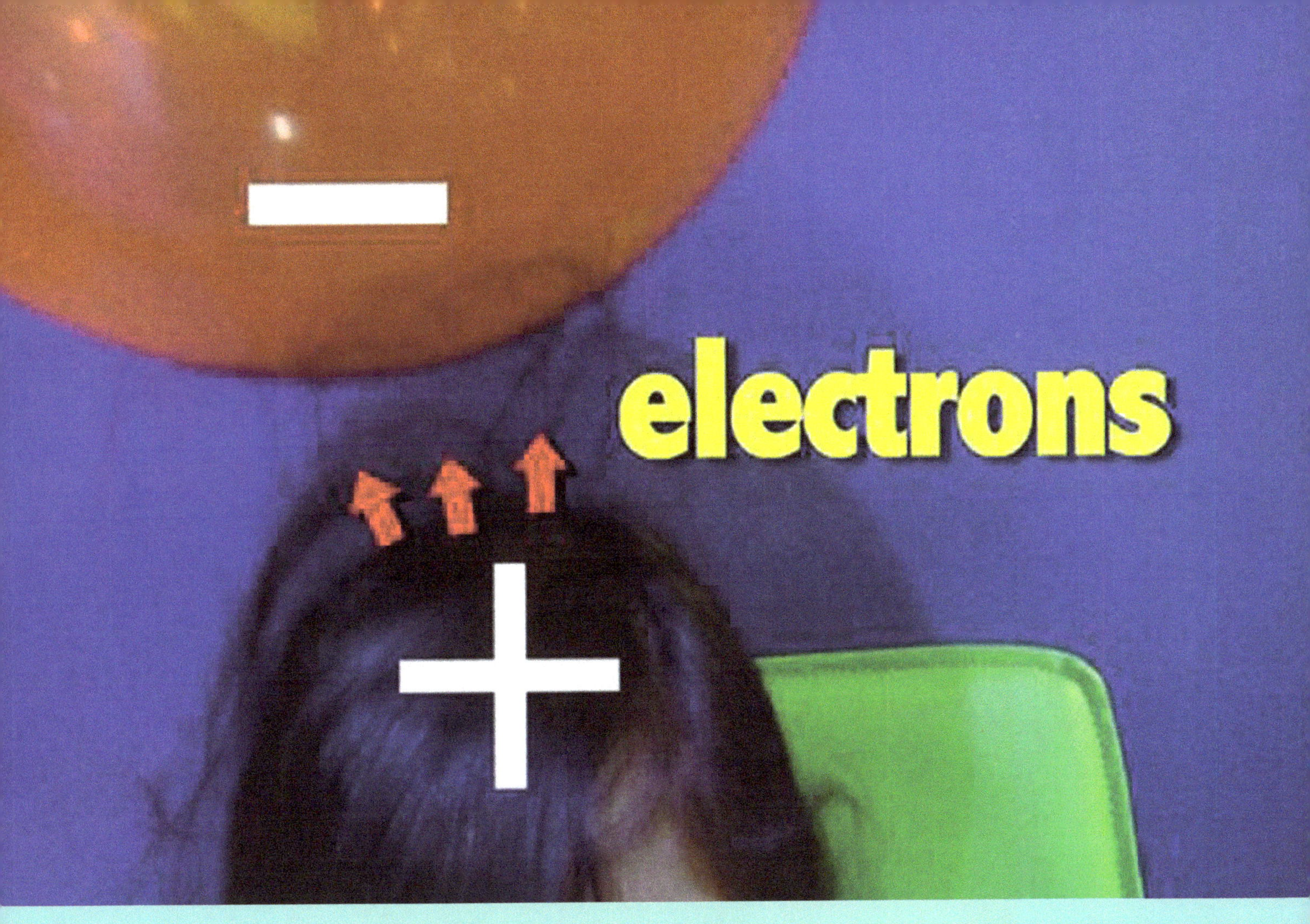

Now the balloon will attract positively charged items and repel negatively charged items. Here are some projects to do so you can see the effects of static electricity. Make sure an adult is supervising whenever you do experiments!

FUN WITH CEREAL

Things You'll Need

- A small comb, one that is made out of rubber or plastic
- Some thread
- Small pieces of dry cereal like Cheerios
- A piece of cloth

STEPS TO TAKE

Take a piece of thread about 12 inches long and tie the cereal piece to it. Tie the other end of the thread to a place where it's not close to anything else. Make sure the comb is completely clean. Wash it and dry it so no water residue is left on it.

THREAD

Now, make the comb "magnetic" by running it through your hair numerous times or by rubbing it back and forth on a piece of cloth. Next, position the charged comb near the cereal.

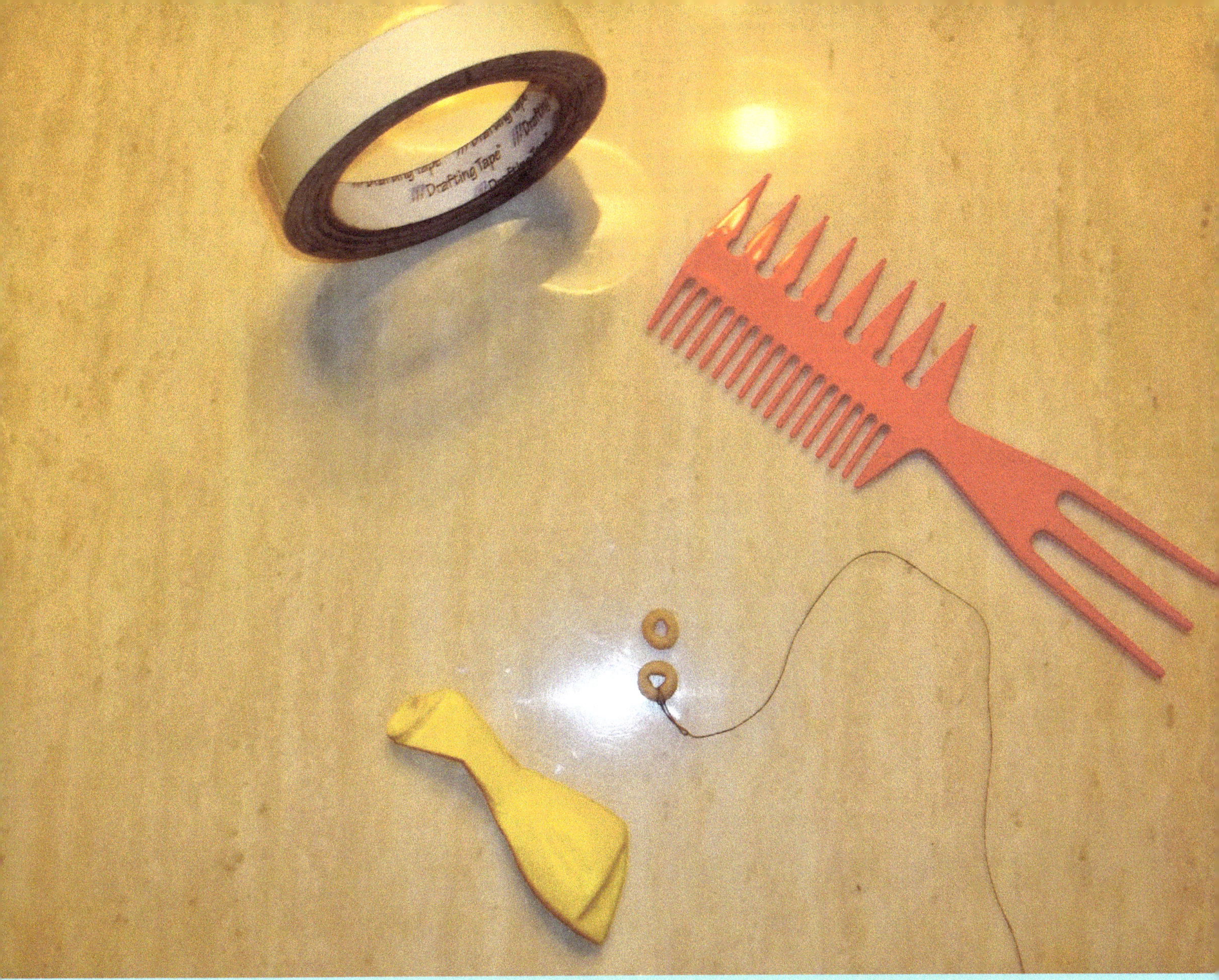

The piece of cereal should swing to tap the comb. Hold the comb completely still until the cereal is repelled away by itself.

WHAT HAPPENED

When you ran the comb through your hair, electrons moved from your head to the surface of the comb. That gave the comb a charge of negative static electricity. The cereal, which was neutral, was attracted to the charge, but when they touched, electrons traveled off the comb to the piece of cereal. Then, both objects, the comb and the cereal, were negatively charged so they repelled each other after they touched.

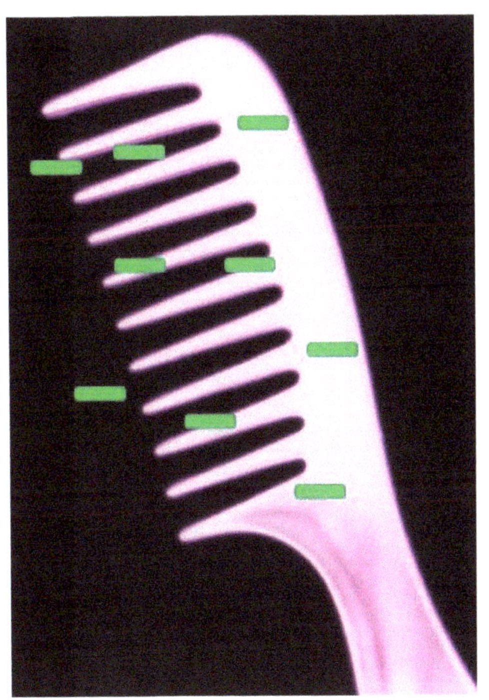

ELECTRONS MOVED FROM HEAD TO COMB

LET'S BEND WATER

Things You'll Need

- A small comb, one that is made out of rubber or plastic
- A sink
- A water faucet

STEPS TO TAKE

Turn on the water faucet. Let the water come out in a small, but steady stream about 1/8 inch in thickness. Make sure the comb is clean and dry. Run it through your hair many times or use a sweater or piece of cloth to rub it. Position the comb near the water and watch what happens. The water should bend slightly near the comb.

WATER BENDING

WHAT HAPPENED

The water, which had a neutral charge, was attracted to the comb, which had been negatively charged. This is the reason the water stretched toward the comb.

LIGHT A BULB

Things You'll Need

- A small comb, one that is made out of rubber or plastic
- A room that's dark
- A light bulb, the fluorescent type

Safety Caution: Do NOT use a wall outlet for this light bulb experiment. Handle the light bulb carefully to avoid breaking it.

STEPS TO TAKE

Take the comb and the fluorescent light bulb into a room that's dark. Make sure you're using a comb that's clean and completely dry. Charge the plastic or rubber comb by using your hair or by rubbing it with a sweater or cloth.

Do it vigorously so that you build up a lot of charge for this experiment. Tap the negatively charged comb to the outside of the fluorescent light bulb and observe closely. The static electricity from the comb should create a few sparks inside the light bulb.

LIGHT BULB

WHAT HAPPENED?

The negatively charged comb moved some of its electrons to the bulb, which caused the tiny sparks of light. When you have a light bulb in a lamp, the electrons that cause the bulb to light up come from the flow of electricity through the power lines traveling through a wire within the bulb.

FUN WITH CHARGED BALLOONS

Things You'll Need

- ⮑ Two different balloons
- ⮑ A fuzzy sweater
- ⮑ Some assorted materials of different types, tissue paper of different sizes, paper and cardboard scraps, yarn or string, a pom pom, some pipe cleaners, ribbon, some different types of cloth, and some packing peanuts

STEPS TO TAKE

Gather up all the materials that you'll need for this experiment. Then, blow up the balloons. Touch one of the balloons to each of the materials you've gathered. Touch the balloons to each other. Next, rub the balloon on the fuzzy sweater. Now touch the balloon to each of the materials and record your findings.

WHAT HAPPENED?

When you first touched the balloon to the objects everything was neutral so nothing happened. However, once the balloon is charged with static electricity, several things may happen.

Some objects, such as the tissue paper, will be attracted to the balloon and will stick to it. Some objects may make a popping sound when they get close to the balloon. Others will be attracted to the balloon, but will weigh too much to stay on it and will fall back down again.

RUBBING THE BALLOON TO
CREATE STATIC ELECTRICITY

HIGH WIRE GRAPEFRUIT
GRAPEFRUIT PALE ALE
ALUMINUM CANS

THE MAGIC ALUMINUM CAN

Things You'll Need

- A PVC pipe
- A cloth
- An aluminum can

STEPS TO TAKE

Rub the PVC pipe with the cloth several times. Place the aluminum can on its side on a flat table and make sure that it stops moving. Without touching the can, bring the pipe close to the can and then move it away slowly. The can should begin moving toward the pipe as if the pipe were magnetic.

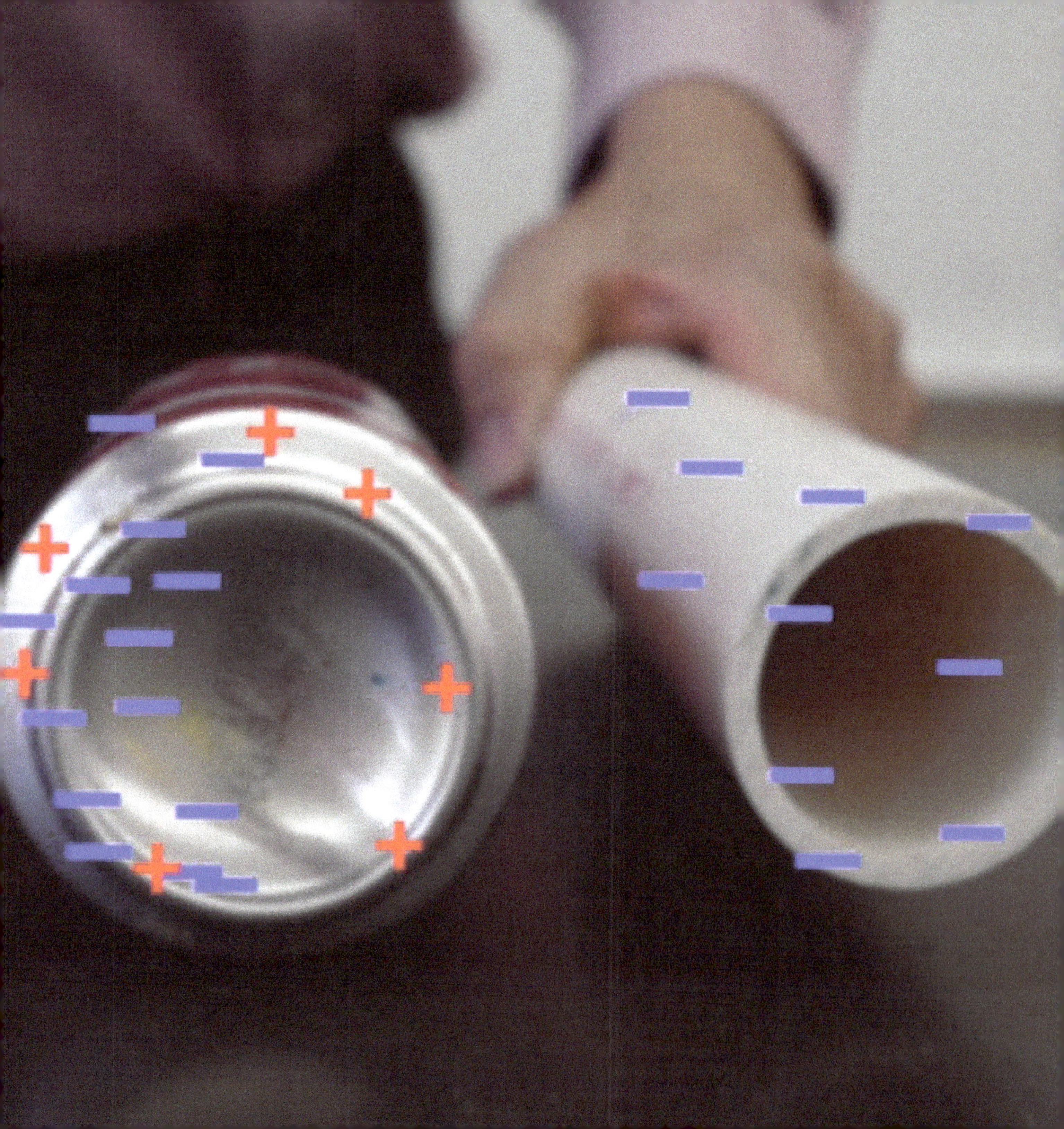

WHAT HAPPENED?

By rubbing the PVC pipe with the cloth, you've piled electrons on it. The extra electrons attract the protons in the aluminum can, so it moves toward the pipe.

THE MOVING BUBBLE

Things You'll Need

- A PVC pipe
- A cloth
- Bubble solution, the type you use with a bubble blower
- A straw for blowing
- A polycarbonate sheet, a strong plastic sheet, which is clear like glass

POLYCARBONATE SHEET

STEPS TO TAKE

Set the polycarbonate sheet on a flat table. Pour some of the bubble solution across the sheet and spread it thinly. Using the straw, blow air into the solution to make a big bubble. Take the cloth and rub it up and down on the PVC pipe to charge it. Place the PVC pipe close to the bubble and watch as the bubble moves toward the pipe. Try this with two bubbles and watch as they move toward the pipe and then burst.

WHAT HAPPENED?

When you took the PVC pipe and rubbed it with the cloth, you got some of the electrons moving. Once the PVC pipe was negatively charged, it attracted the positively charged protons in the soap bubbles.

PIPE BUBBLES

THE DANCING BALLS

Things You'll Need

- ➲ Tiny styrofoam balls, about 10
- ➲ Aluminum foil
- ➲ Four small wooden blocks
- ➲ A cloth
- ➲ A polycarbonate sheet, a strong plastic sheet which is clear like glass
- ➲ Top of a cardboard box that is about an inch deep
- ➲ A sheet of fabric that fits in the cardboard box top

STEPS TO TAKE

Wrap the tiny styrofoam balls in small pieces of aluminum foil so they are completely covered. Place the box top on a table so that the flat side is against the table and the "open" side is up. Place the cloth in the box and place a sheet of aluminum foil on top of the cloth. Place the wooden blocks in the corners of the box top and place the polycarbonate sheet on top. Now you should have a stage for your dance to begin.

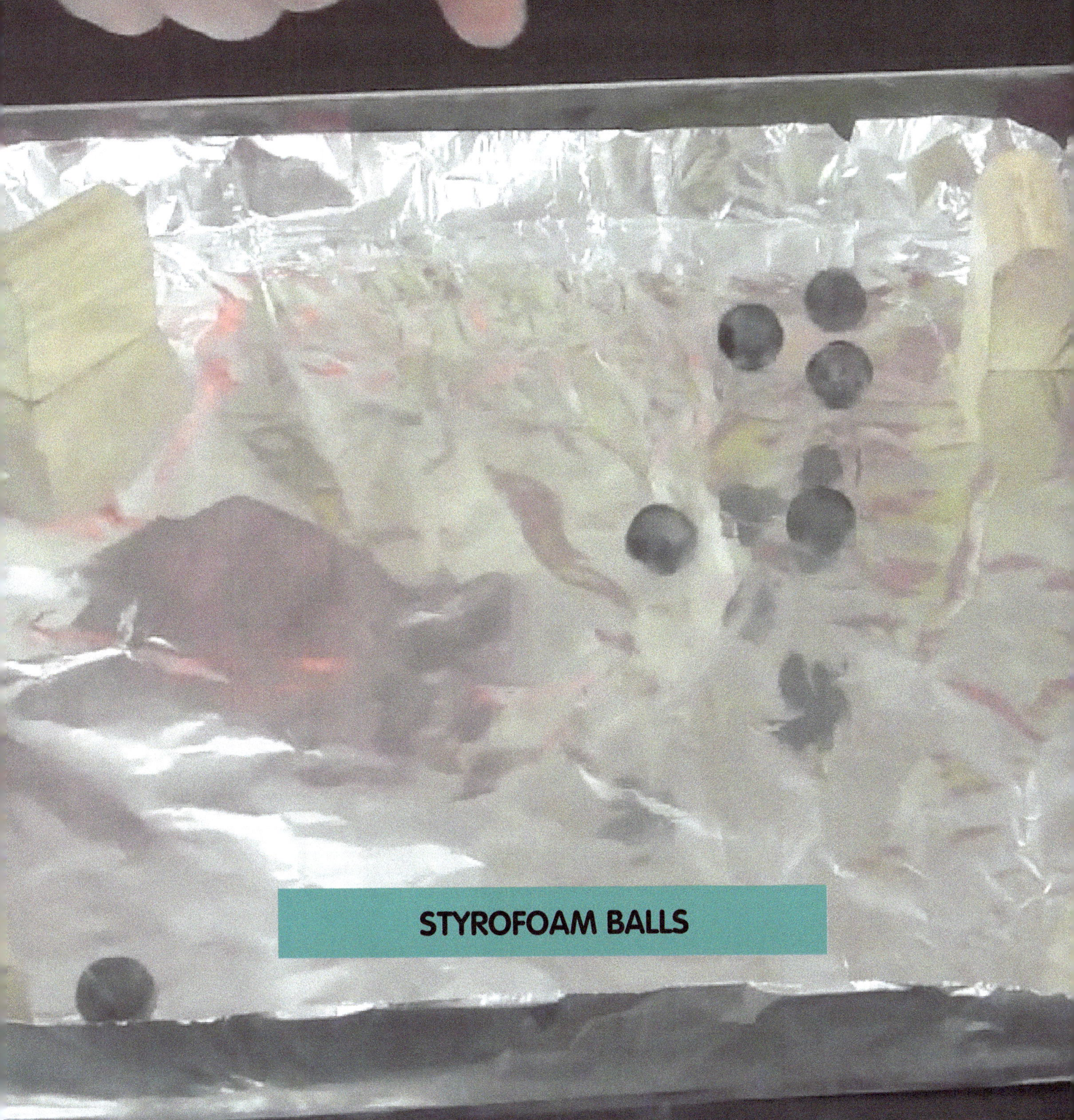
STYROFOAM BALLS

ELECTRICAL CURRENT

Next, rub the top of the polycarbonate sheet with a cloth vigorously. Place one of the aluminum wrapped balls on the polycarbonate sheet. If you place your finger near the ball it will repel it, so the ball will now "dance" around. Now take the polycarbonate sheet off and dump the balls into the box. Put the polycarbonate sheet back on top. Now you can use your finger to make the balls dance.

WHAT HAPPENED

When you placed the balls in the box, they were attracted to the negatively charged polycarbonate sheet. The balls will continue to move until their charges and the charges of the sheet are back in balance.

DANCING BALLS EXPERIMENT

SLIDE CREATING STATIC ELECTRICITY

STATIC HAPPENS!

Static electricity happens when there's an imbalance between the negative and positive electrical charges either in an object or on its surface. The charge remains in place or "static" until it's able to discharge to another object. A charged object has extra electrons so it can attract the protons in another object. You'll notice a lot of instances of static electricity in your home or school, especially on cold, dry days.

Awesome! Now that you know more about how static electricity behaves, you can read more about the physics behind electricity and magnetism in the Baby Professor book Physics for Kids: Electricity and Magnetism.

Visit
BABY PROFESSOR
EDUCATION KIDS
www.BabyProfessorBooks.com
to download Free Baby Professor eBooks
and view our catalog of new and exciting
Children's Books